What To Do When Someone Dies:

The Nine Phases of Administration

Table of Contents

The Death I Never Expected

Wednesday, April 13, 2005, at 5:30 p.m. I received a phone call from my daughter-in-law. She was blunt. The first words out of her mouth were, "RYAN'S BEEN SHOT." The only detail she had was the location of a store parking lot where she last saw him an hour before. Little did she know it would be the last time she saw him alive.

Ryan was transported to Huntington Memorial Hospital in Pasadena. The next thing I knew, I was at the hospital. I asked at the front desk where I would find my son, Ryan. I was informed someone would be out to talk to me. I was ushered into a sterile hall where I leaned up against the wall, and the chaplain told me, RYAN, MY FIRST BORN, was dead. He died of seven gunshots. I asked if I could see him, and I was informed that was not a good idea.

Today, in my mind's eye, I see him lying on a table full of holes and covered in blood. On another occasion, in my mind's eye, I saw the impact of each of the seven shots.

That day, the journey I had been on for years changed. I am an attorney who has been involved in estate planning and estate administration since the early 1970s. I now understand in a more meaningful way what an individual goes through when they lose a loved one.

What To Do When Someone Dies

It is a journey that every family will go through. I found it was like being dropped in the middle of a lake of tar, and the only way out was with the help of others. Once you got on dryland, with each step you took, another drop of gooey tar fell off your clothes into spots on the ground. Eventually, most of that gooey tar had fallen off, and you were now walking into a new normal.

This tragedy provided me with a fresh perspective of what estate administration means to a family.

Today, one of my main goals is to help people get out of that lake of tar and begin their walk to a new normal. One thing that I have found that helps is to share with them the nine reasons, which are the same as the nine phases of every estate administration. I have found that when they know what to expect and why it has to be taken care of, they can find that new normal sooner and with less emotional trauma.

What To Do When Someone Dies

Eighteen years and four months later, Ryan's son is finishing his first week of the Marine Corps boot camp. Aiden never met his father; he just sent a letter to his mother that was shared with the family after his first week. The comment was made that it was very difficult to read his handwriting, just like his father Ryan's handwriting was difficult to read. Somebody else added that they could not read my handwriting either, and it must be a Brock trait.

I want them to know that the handwriting of both of my parents was very legible.

I share the story of Ryan's death during the first meeting with individuals who have lost their loved one and now must deal with settling the estate, the dreaded Probate. Even though a living trust was prepared and, therefore, they avoided the dreaded Probate, there are still many loose ends that need to be tied up.

As a result of this experience, I discovered when taking care of my son's small estate that I performed essentially the same tasks as the million-dollar estates that I have assisted families in settling.

Their most common question is: Why do we have Probate, or what is necessary to settle the estate for which we have a trust?

In answer, I share with them the nine phases of estate administration.

The Nine Phases

Phase One
Find a Law Firm to Review Estate Planning Documents

Phase Two
Prepare and Sign Documents

Phase Three
Identify All the Assests

Phase Four
Figure Out Who Is Owed What

Phase Five
Decide Who Gets What and When

Phase Six
Deal with Tax Returns and IRS

Phase Seven
Report All Actions Done

Phase Eight
Give Assests to Those Who Should Receive Them

Phase Nine
Close Administration

However, before we go into more detail about the nine phases, we need to explain the two main cases these phases affect:

Probate and Trust Administration.

Probate	A Probate happens when someone dies, and there is no Trust. Even if there is a Will; without a Trust, that entire estate will need to go through Probate. A Probate tends to take longer than a Trust Administration and generally costs more in court and legal fees.
Trust Administration	A Trust Administration happens when someone dies, and they had a Trust properly prepared. A Trust Administration generally takes less time and costs less than a Probate.

Phase One: Find a Law Firm to Review Estate Planning Documents

This phase involves the initial contact between us and the family member taking charge of the situation. Sometimes, this meeting includes multiple family members of the decedent so we can determine who will be the Personal Representative or Executor. The Personal Representative is the person in charge of helping the attorney administer the Probate or Trust Administration for the family. This person is often a member of the family of the decedent. The first order of business is reviewing the Trust or Will, or discussing what will happen if there is no Will.

During this phase, we will review:

- All estate plans, trusts, and/or wills and any other estate planning documents
- All bank statements, deeds, and other documents reflecting the date of death title of the decedent's assets.
- All liabilities of the decedent
- All family information, including the names, addresses, and telephone numbers of the decedent's spouse, children, parents, and brothers and sisters.
- Contact information for everyone named in the estate planning documents.
- Any issues regarding family dynamics or concerns about potential conflicts
- Whether any probate administration or court petitions are required before the Personal Representative can take charge of the Trust assets.

This review is very critical because often tax laws change, and important decisions must be made in a timely manner to minimize taxes.

From the very start of the administration, the Personal Representative should keep a detailed timesheet of all time spent during the administration. Most Trust Administrations and Probates allow for compensation to the Personal Representative, so keeping records of all the time spent acting as the Personal Representative will be essential to determine the amount of compensation.

Further, since the Personal Representative will be required to account to the Trust Beneficiaries, the Personal Representative should hire a bookkeeper for the Trust and keep detailed records of all income and expenses of the Trust. The law requires that the Personal Representative act with the utmost care in administering the Trust and imposes many duties upon the Personal Representative, which we will review with you.

Phase Two: Prepare and Sign Documents

During this phase, we will prepare the necessary documents so that the Personal Representative can be legally appointed to take charge of the Trust assets. The Personal Representative will use the authority to wind up the decedent's affairs and to transfer the assets to the heirs and beneficiaries named in the Trust.

All assets will be retitled into the name of the Personal Representative on behalf of the Trust. If Court involvement is needed, we will file documents to obtain the necessary approval.

If you have a will or no estate planning documents, then depending upon the size of the estate, a Probate filed with the court will be required.

In Utah, it could be informal or formal Probate, and it does not depend upon the size of the estate, whether it's formal or informal. It will depend on factors that are generally best understood by an attorney who is knowledgeable in the area of probate law and experienced.

In both a formal and informal Probate, the authority is conferred by the court,

and it is referred to as Letters of Administration or Letters Testamentary.

If there is a Trust, you receive the authority to act as the person in charge based on the Trust document itself. The Trust identifies a successor Personal Representative, and what is necessary is the proper legal documents identifying you as the new successor Personal Representative.

With the Trust, your authority is conferred by a Certification of Trust quoting the appropriate sections of the Trust and the probate code and properly signed and executed.

Can You Do All of That By Yourself?

Probably, if you have the time and knowledge on how to search out all the information needed in the probate code and find the required forms or draft the documents. Most people don't have the time or energy to do this on their own. Some try, but often, they end up needing an attorney after struggling to do it alone. So, why should you take upon that headache yourself? Especially when,

The cost of having a qualified, experienced attorney is shared by all the heirs and beneficiaries.

What To Do When Someone Dies

Even when an attorney is assisting you with the amount of work necessary, the challenges you face most likely do not compensate you for your time and aggravation.

What other documents do you need to begin? You're going to need a taxpayer ID number from the IRS. A good attorney will give you a memorandum setting forth your duties as the Personal Representative IE Personal Representative or administrator under the probate code and the trust document.

If it is a Trust Administration, you must give a very particular special notice to all the heirs and beneficiaries of the existence of the Trust, and that notice also places a limit on the amount of time that someone can contest the Trust.

You will begin, if you have not already, gathering the names and addresses of all heirs and beneficiaries. Do you know what the difference is between an heir and a beneficiary? The attorney will help you identify all those individuals.

You will discuss whether the Department of Health, your state taxing authority, or your Department of Corrections needs to be notified of the individual's passing.

You will discuss the importance of locating all bills and creditors of the decedent and which ones you should pay, when you should pay them, and if you do not have to pay them.

You will discuss how to identify and locate all assets of the decedent and then, once you've located them, how to take control of those assets. One of the most important responsibilities and jobs you have is to take control of all assets, determine the value of the assets, and protect those assets.

There are many other specific tasks that may be necessary depending upon the assets and liabilities and family dynamics of an estate administration. You will be at these first two meetings, and you will discuss as many of these as possible. The attorney will begin to give you a road map for your journey down the maze of Probate or Trust Administration.

Phase Three: Identify All the Assets

The Personal Representative will finalize an inventory of all the assets in the Trust. The Personal Representative will also obtain appraisals of all assets to determine the value as of the date of death. The date of death value will affect many tax issues that your tax advisor will address with you.

Review Assets

- Amount
- Type
- Title
- Documents
- All names & addresses

It is important to have a clear and accurate inventory and appraisal of all assets. I've dealt with cases where not every asset is assessed at the beginning, and it almost always leads to problems. At one point, the storage section of my office was filled with client assets because the family could not agree on what the items were worth and who would receive them. By having proper appraisals done on the assets, some of that headache could have been avoided.

Phase Four:
Figure Out Who Is Owed What

After a thorough review of the decedent's files and records, the Personal Representative will determine whether the decedent has any debts. Then, we will advise you about the next steps to address any creditors.

Pay Creditors

Please note that when you start collecting the bills of the deceased, you do not pay any of the bills until after all have been collected and all the assets

have been totaled. If there are not enough assets, there is a priority for payment of claims. That priority is as follows:

- the Personal Representative and their attorney and the cost of administration
- taxes
- secure debt
- unsecured debt
- specific bequest
- the residual to the heirs and beneficiaries

Another reason to make sure to assess all the assets first is that sometimes creditors won't even file a claim. In every case, once all the creditors have been established, we send a formal Notice of Administration as required by statute that gives the creditors four months to formally file a claim. If they don't file that claim in the four months, the creditors are out of luck.

I've had multiple cases where some creditors never file a claim even if the creditors file a claim, the amount can often be reduced. For example, in one of my cases, a creditor made a claim. However, after some negotiation, we were able to reduce the original amount and ended up paying only about $0.25 on the dollar.

Phase Five: Decide Who Gets What And When

After all details of assets and liabilities are ascertained and thoroughly reviewed, the Personal Representative will need to consider how the Trust assets should be distributed to those named in the Trust. Sometimes, certain assets will need to be sold to satisfy the liabilities of the Trust. Other times, assets will need to be sold to avoid co-ownership, which would later create conflict. We often advise the Personal representative to serve a notice on the beneficiaries and obtain their consent before selling any assets. The notice and consent protect the Personal Representative by minimizing potential liability. We will advise the Personal Representative in making these decisions and assist in creating a workable plan for distributing the assets.

I once had a case that was intestate, meaning there was no Will. Unfortunately, one of the children was blind, and she was receiving government benefits. She also had one minor child. If she received her share of the inheritance, she would have lost her government benefits until the inheritance was completely spent.

This is a situation where there should have been planning in advance that would place her inheritance in a Special Needs Trust that would allow her to keep her government benefits and her inheritance. Fortunately, we were able to create a Special Needs Trust for her that allowed her to continue to receive her government benefits and her inheritance, and after 15 years, there are still some assets in the Special Needs Trust. However, because there was no planning in advance, this Special Needs Trust was expensive to set up and it has been expensive to maintain it all of these years. Fortunately, there has been no requirement that an accounting be submitted to the court every year. So she could keep track of her trustee on her own. However, there is a requirement for a bond, and that requires a pre-bond premium to be paid each year.

This is a situation that is much better to plan in advance than after the fact. It is a situation, though, that requires analysis after you have gathered all the assets and the debts and then evaluate how to distribute those assets.

Phase Six:
Deal with Tax Returns and IRS

The Personal Representative's tax advisor will prepare the final tax returns and assess whether an estate tax return needs to be filed. Final tax returns are necessary for the last year of the decedent's life and at the end of the administration. After the IRS and the Franchise Tax Board approve the tax returns, the estate can close.

Years ago, I had a probate, and the decedent, who was over 90 when he passed away, did not have a Social Security number. Therefore, his final tax returns could not be filed. However, the personal representative was responsible for filing that return, and if taxes were owing could have been held responsible for paying those taxes. As a result, we needed to leave the probate estate open for over ten years until the statute of limitations expired.

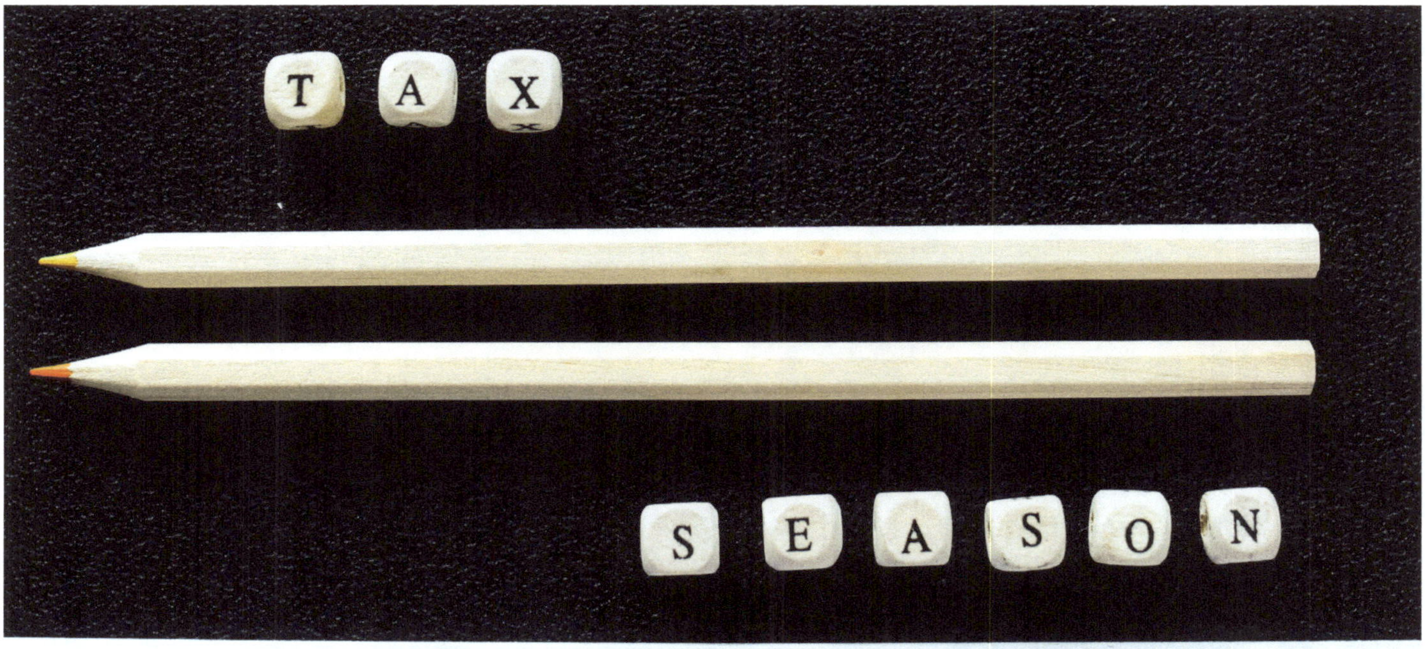

What To Do When Someone Dies

Because the Personal Representative could be individually responsible for filing and paying state and federal income taxes, it is very important that the attorney advises the Personal Representative to meet with a CPA or other tax professional who has experience preparing fiduciary tax returns.

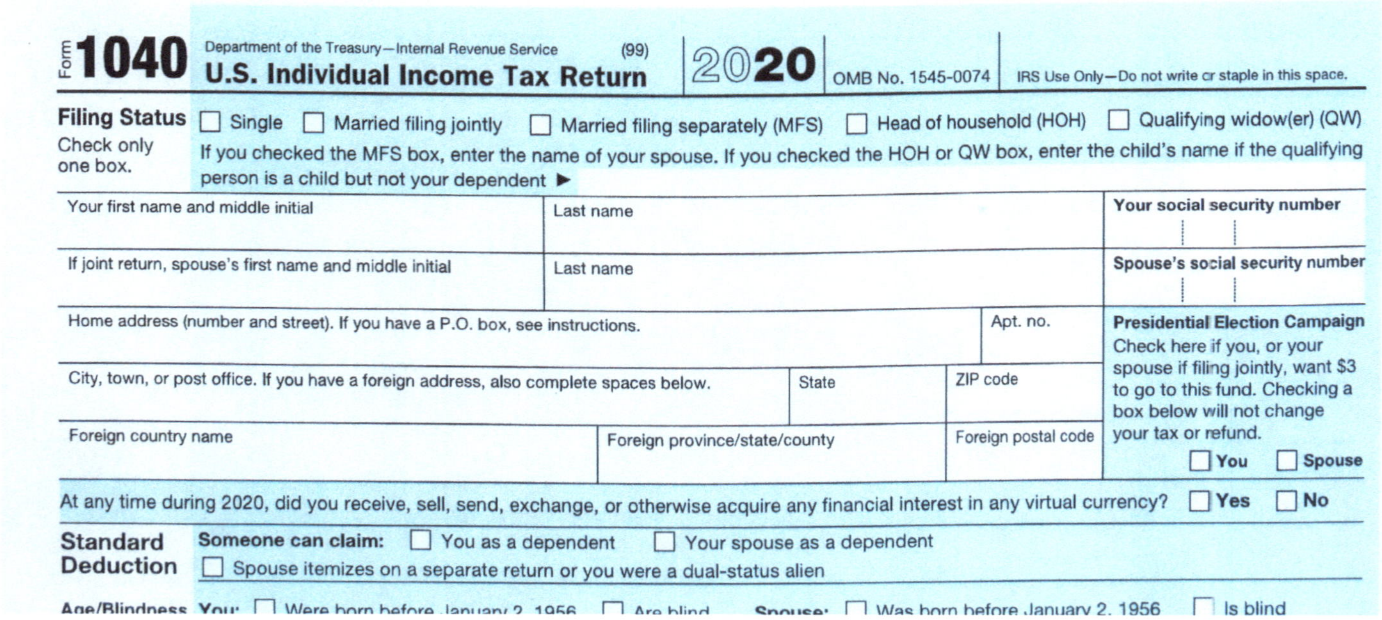

Form **1040** Department of the Treasury—Internal Revenue Service (99)
U.S. Individual Income Tax Return **2020** OMB No. 1545-0074 IRS Use Only—Do not write or staple in this space.

Filing Status Check only one box.
☐ Single ☐ Married filing jointly ☐ Married filing separately (MFS) ☐ Head of household (HOH) ☐ Qualifying widow(er) (QW)
If you checked the MFS box, enter the name of your spouse. If you checked the HOH or QW box, enter the child's name if the qualifying person is a child but not your dependent ▶

Your first name and middle initial	Last name			**Your social security number**
If joint return, spouse's first name and middle initial	Last name			**Spouse's social security number**
Home address (number and street). If you have a P.O. box, see instructions.			Apt. no.	**Presidential Election Campaign** Check here if you, or your spouse if filing jointly, want $3 to go to this fund. Checking a box below will not change your tax or refund. ☐ **You** ☐ **Spouse**
City, town, or post office. If you have a foreign address, also complete spaces below.		State	ZIP code	
Foreign country name	Foreign province/state/county		Foreign postal code	

At any time during 2020, did you receive, sell, send, exchange, or otherwise acquire any financial interest in any virtual currency? ☐ **Yes** ☐ **No**

Standard Deduction **Someone can claim:** ☐ You as a dependent ☐ Your spouse as a dependent
☐ Spouse itemizes on a separate return or you were a dual-status alien

Not everyone files their taxes in a timely manner, and it is the Personal Representative's responsibility to ensure that all tax returns are filed and taxes are paid. Sometimes, that can be a very complicated, long, and drawn-out process when working with the IRS.

Phase Seven:
Report All Actions Done

During Phase #7, we will advise you about preparing the required accounting for the Trust beneficiaries. The accounting typically includes a report of all assets on hand on the date of death, receipts, disbursements, and any distributions during the administration. This report is required by law to be given to all heirs and beneficiaries. The report will also need to include all compensation paid to the Personal Representative.

Some states and many Revocable Living Trusts require that the Personal Representative deliver a report setting out the primary work accomplished by the Personal Representative, listing the assets and the liabilities of the decedent, and an accounting setting forth the values income received, expenses paid, and distribution to all of the heirs and beneficiaries.

Even if it is not required, it is a good practice for the Personal Representative to provide such a report to all heirs and beneficiaries because the actions of the Personal Representative are generally questioned, or there are concerns about what they have done, and without such a report oftentimes there can become a conflict.

Lack of information creates unrest that can result in someone suspecting that the Personal Representative has not done their duty properly and perhaps has taken advantage of the decedent's estate.

In a Trust Administration a number of years ago, after evaluating all the assets and dividing the assets between the survivor's Trust and the decedent's Trust, we then sent a report to all the heirs and beneficiaries. That report gave all parties a deadline to object to the work of the trustee. No one objected, and we distributed all the assets according to the terms of the Trust. Well, three years later, one of the heirs of the Trust claimed that the Trust Administration was done improperly. Their claim did not go anywhere because of the notice given in the report.

It is very important to provide a complete report to all the heirs and beneficiaries to reduce the chances that they will complain about the administration later. If you are concerned about the possibility that they will complain, the next step is to ask for court approval of your work as trustee.

Phase Eight: Give Assets to Those Who Should Receive Them

Once the Personal Representative calculates the final costs and fees, we will assist the Personal Representative in finalizing a distribution agreement to memorialize the distribution of assets to the named beneficiaries, showing the valuation of each beneficiary's share. During this phase, the Personal Representative will also be paid compensation as allowed by the Trust. Typically, we will prepare a Release for the beneficiaries to sign in order to minimize the Personal representative's liability.

Distribution can be quite a challenge when the distribution takes place many years after the death. One Probate included distribution to well over 40 individuals because the decedent passed away almost 50 years before the Probate was brought to court. He had sixteen children, thirteen of whom lived to adulthood, but not all of them had children. However, some of those who lived to adulthood and had children and had passed away before the probate was commenced. Therefore, we had to find all of the descendants of these individuals and then make a distribution to them and obtain receipts for filing with the court.

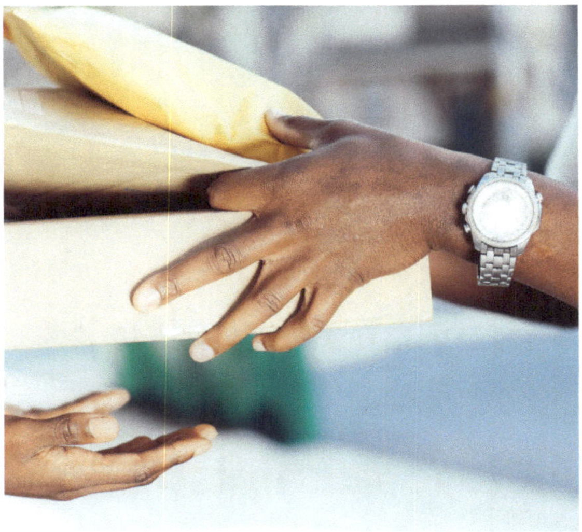

Phase #9: Close Administration

Upon distributing all the Trust assets, the Personal Representative will need to obtain receipts of distribution from each heir or beneficiary. We will also provide instructions for any ongoing trusts, and then the administration of the Trust can be closed.

In Probate, the court requires all beneficiaries to sign a receipt and have it filed with the court before the probate personal representative can be discharged. On more than one occasion, beneficiaries have either been slow or refused to sign receipts. Fortunately, we've proved to the court that they were paid by submitting a copy of the canceled check. We had that canceled check because the attorney made distribution through his attorney trust account. Again, just a little tip to facilitate closing the estate.

Obtain Receipts

Provide Instructions

Close Administration

Fees

During the initial meeting, which took place at Phase 1, we will discuss our process for assisting you, the estimated time to complete the administration, and what you can expect the fees to be. Our general practice for fees differs from most law firms, which charge by the hour and incur additional costs for every telephone call made. Rather, we calculate the fee based on our experience, the amount of time required to complete the work, and any unusual situations that may arise. We will need to apply our experience and expertise to the matter in a way that benefits you the most.

Due to the unique nature of each case, fees may vary. This means that we cannot give you an accurate estimate of the fee until we meet. However, we can make sure that by the time you leave your first meeting with us, you have an accurate estimate of the final fees to expect.

This process of determining fees enables us to provide each client with the personalized assistance they require, without the client having to worry about money.

What Now?

Now that you've read through "What to Do When Someone Dies," you might have some questions. That is completely normal. We don't expect you to become an expert on this overnight. That is where we come in. Proven Law has been helping people navigate this difficult in their lives for over 20 years in the Southern Utah area. We can do the same for you. Below, we left some space for you to write down any questions or concerns you want to talk about concerning this document or anything else that has to do with Estate Planning in general. We hope to hear from you soon.

Authors

E. Lawrence Brock

E. Lawrence Brock, "Larry," was born and raised in Los Angeles, growing up in the shadow of downtown during the 50s and 60s. He attended California State University, Los Angeles, and then Southwestern University School of Law, graduating in 1979 with a Juris Doctorate.

He is married to Joyce, and they have eight children, each having three when they married in 1987, and they added two more.

For most of his life, he lived in Southern California, and in 2015, he and Joyce moved to St. George, Utah, to be 350 miles closer to most of their grandchildren, and where there is no snow. Those grandchildren live in Utah along 100 miles of the snowy Wasatch Front.

ProvenLaw

ProvenLaw has served the Southern Utah Area for over 20 years. We offer unmatched expertise backed by over 90 years of collective experience. Our primary goal is to assist our clients in finding the ideal solution for themselves and their families.

We strive to provide an environment where our clients feel comfortable and can entrust us with personal and often heartbreaking information.

As our main focus is Estate Planning, we consistently deal with people during one of the most difficult times of their lives: the death of a loved one or planning for their own death. It is not lost on us the faith and trust our clients must give us. As such, we work diligently to make sure your legal plan is tailored to your specific needs and is perfect for you.

www.ingramcontent.com/pod-product-compliance
Lightning Source LLC
LaVergne TN
LVHW070230061026
849616LV00024B/81
* 9 7 8 1 7 3 6 1 0 5 2 3 8 *